CHRISTOPHER DANIELSON

Which One Doesn't Belong?

Playing with Shapes

Charlesbridge

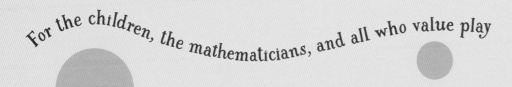

For the children, the mathematicians, and all who value play

First trade edition 2019
Copyright © 2016 by
Christopher Danielson

All rights reserved, including the right of
reproduction in whole or in part in any
form. Charlesbridge and colophon are
registered trademarks of Charlesbridge
Publishing, Inc.

At the time of publication, all URLs
printed in this book were accurate and
active. Charlesbridge and the author
are not responsible for the content or
accessibility of any website.

Published by Charlesbridge
85 Main Street
Watertown, MA 02472
(617) 926-0329
www.charlesbridge.com

First published in 2016 by Stenhouse
Publishers • www.stenhouse.com

Library of Congress Cataloging-in-Publication Data
Names: Danielson, Christopher, author.
  | Previously published as: Danielson,
  Christopher. Which one doesn't
  belong?: a shapes book.
Title: Which one doesn't belong?: playing
  with shapes/Christopher Danielson.
Other titles: Which one does not belong
Description: First trade edition. |
  Watertown, MA: Charlesbridge, 2019.
Identifiers: LCCN 2018003341 (print) |
  LCCN 2018010131 (ebook) |
  ISBN 9781632898111 (ebook) |
  ISBN 9781632898128 (ebook pdf) |
  ISBN 9781580899444 (reinforced
  for library use) |
  ISBN 9781580899468 (softcover)
Subjects: LCSH: Shapes—Juvenile
  literature. | Geometry—Juvenile
  literature. | Mathematics—Study and
  teaching (Elementary)
Classification: LCC QA445.5 (ebook) |
  LCC QA445.5 .D37 2018 (print) |
  DDC 516/.15—dc23
LC record available at https://lccn.loc
  .gov/2018003341

Printed in China
(hc) 10 9 8 7 6 5 4 3 2 1
(sc) 10 9 8 7 6 5 4 3 2 1

Display type set in Myster Bold by
  Denis Serebryakov
Text type set in Grenadine MVB by
  Markanna Studios Inc.
Printed by 1010 Printing International
  Limited in Huizhou, Guangdong,
  China
Production supervision by
  Brian G. Walker
Designed by Tom Morgan
  (www.bluedes.com) and
  Joyce White

This book is **different** from other books about shapes. Every page asks the same question, and every answer can be correct.

Turn the page to see for yourself.

Look at these shapes. There are many ways they are alike and different. Pick out a shape that seems different from the others.

Which one doesn't belong?

Why?

Did you choose the shape in the **lower left**? If you did, maybe it's because this shape **isn't colored in**.

Did you choose the shape in the **lower right**? If you did, maybe it's because this is the only shape that **looks like it's leaning over.**

Or maybe you said that this shape doesn't belong because it has **three sides**, and the others have four.

Some people choose this shape because it's **the only square.**

Other people say that this shape doesn't belong because its **angles are the wrong size.**

All of these answers are correct!
On every page of this book, you can choose any shape and say that it doesn't belong.

The important thing is to have a reason **why**.

Some pages are more challenging than others. You may need to put the book down and come back later.

When you're ready, turn the page and decide:

Which one doesn't belong?

Which one doesn't belong?

Which one doesn't belong?

Which one
doesn't
belong?

Which one doesn't belong?

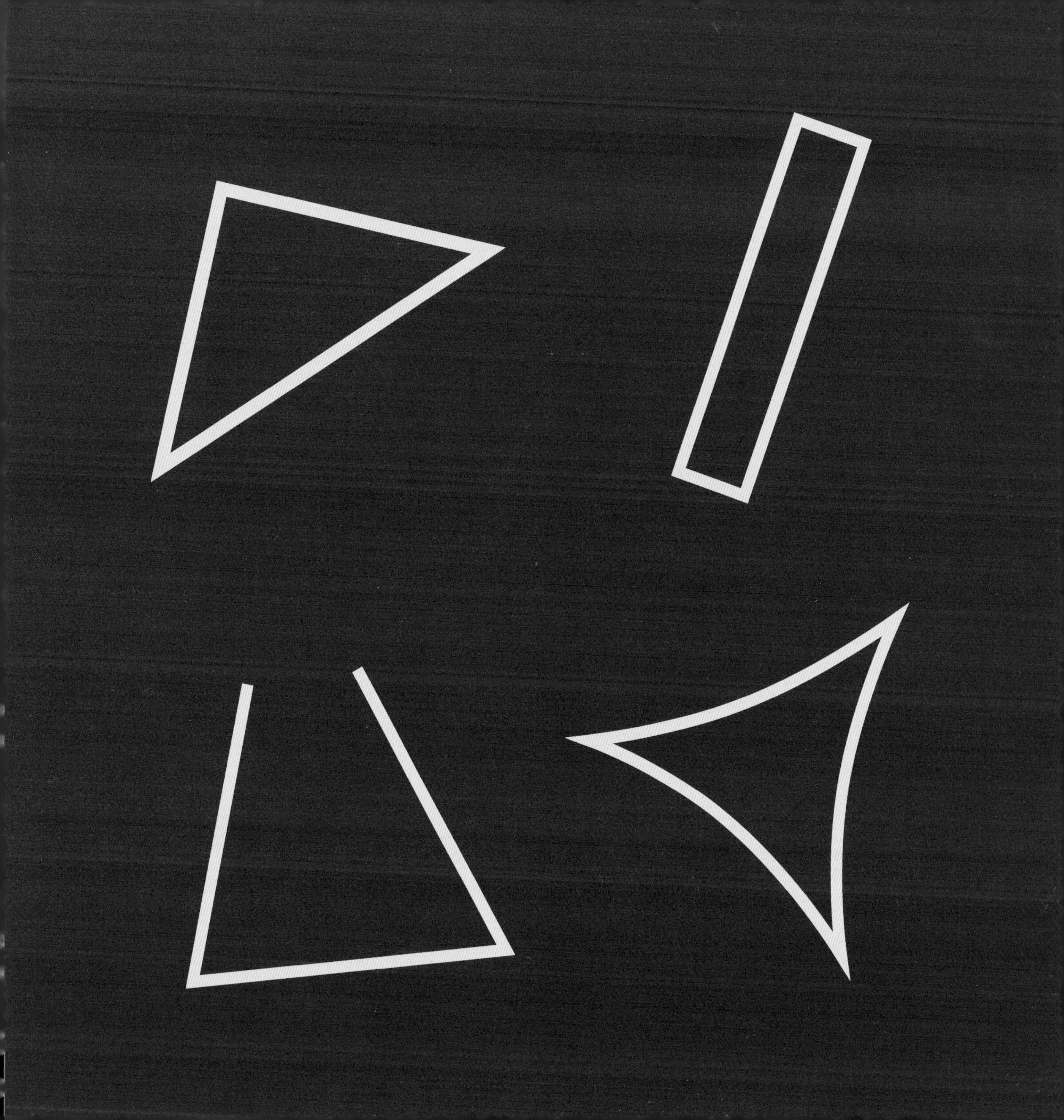

Which one doesn't belong?

Which one doesn't belong?

Which one doesn't belong?

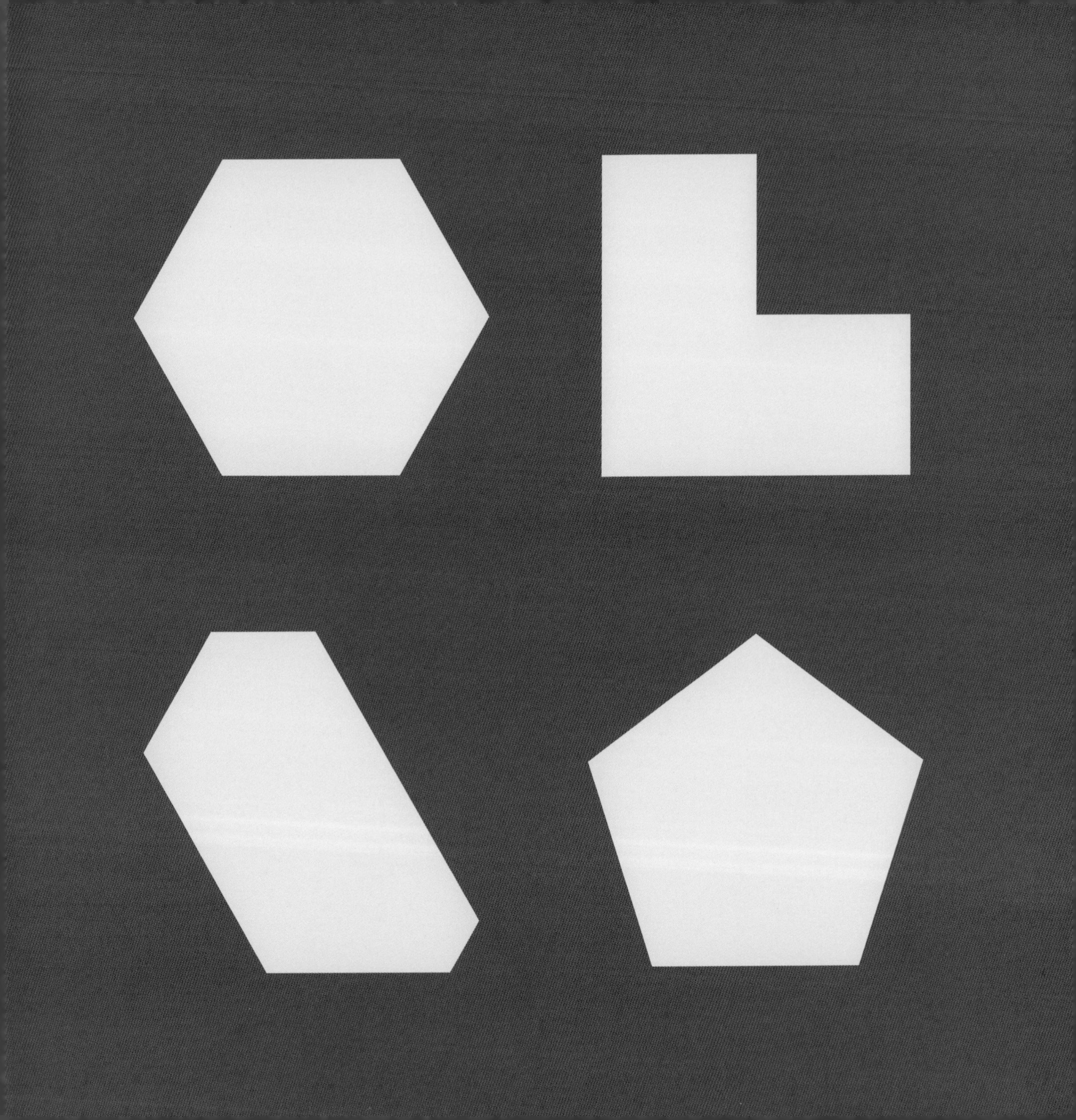

Which one doesn't belong?

Which one doesn't belong?

Which one doesn't belong?

Dear Reader,

As you talk about which shapes don't belong, have fun! Don't worry about being "right."

All properties count here; all ideas matter.

A triangle is like a square because they both have straight sides. But if you count the number of sides, they are different. You're thinking in a mathy way when you notice sameness and difference for one property at a time.

The properties are more important than the words you use to describe them. If you use words such as *smooshed*, *stretched*, *bent*, *dented*, *curvy*, *colored in*, or *cupcake* while reading this book, you're probably doing some great math!

—Christopher